Classroom Helpers

Parts of Speech

Grade 3

By
Sara Freemen

Cover Design by
Ron Kauffman

Cover Illustration by
Duane Bibby

Inside Illustrations by
Various Artists

Published by Frank Schaffer Publications
an imprint of

Credits

Author: Sara Freeman
Cover Design: Ron Kauffman
Cover Illustration: Duane Bibby
Inside Illustrations: Various Artists
Project Director/Editor: Jeanine Manfro
Editors: Angella Phebus, Mary Hassinger, Sara Bierling
Page Design: Wayne Newton
Page Production: Kruse Graphic Design, Ron Kauffman

McGraw-Hill
Children's Publishing

A Division of The ***McGraw-Hill*** *Companies*

Published by Frank Schaffer Publications
An imprint of McGraw-Hill Children's Publishing

Send all inquiries to:
McGraw-Hill Children's Publishing
3195 Wilson Drive NW
Grand Rapids, Michigan 49544

Parts of Speech—grade 3
ISBN: 0-7682-0834-3

1 2 3 4 5 6 7 8 9 07 06 05 04 03 02

Name ______________________ Date ____________

What Doesn't Belong?

A noun names a person, place, or thing.
Doctor, **farm**, **giraffe**, and **chair** are all nouns.

Read each set of words.
Cross out the word that is not a noun.
Write a new noun to match the set.

1.	~~visited~~	village	community	town	city
2.	brother	cousin	happy	aunt	______
3.	tiger	hunted	cheetah	leopard	______
4.	planet	far	star	asteroid	______
5.	sleet	hail	rain	cloudy	______
6.	lawyer	teacher	painter	slower	______
7.	butterfly	tiny	grasshopper	ant	______
8.	paper	pencil	carefully	scissors	______
9.	drove	truck	scooter	bike	______
10.	loud	flute	saxophone	violin	______
11.	library	bank	restaurant	beside	______
12.	nickel	spends	penny	quarter	______
13.	dog	cat	hamster	please	______
14.	stomach	brain	healthy	lungs	______
15.	clever	fairy	elf	monster	______
16.	lake	swims	ocean	stream	______

Name ______________________________ Date ________________

What Is Your Favorite . . . ?

A common noun names any person, place, or thing.

A proper noun names a special person, place, or thing. It begins with a capital letter.

Underline the common noun. Write a matching proper noun to finish the sentence.

1. I think Wentworth is a great school.
2. My teacher is ______________________.

3. I like to play with my friends, especially ______________ and ______________.
4. One person whom I admire is ______________________.
5. ______________________ is a big city.
6. The state I would most like to visit is ______________________.
7. If I had a dog, I would name it ______________________.
8. ______________________ is my favorite book character.
9. My favorite author is ______________________.

10. ______________________ is the current U.S. President.
11. My street is ______________________.

12. I was born during the month of ______________________.
13. My favorite holiday is ______________________.
14. ______________________ is a very tall mountain.
15. I hope to travel to ______________________, my favorite planet.

Name ______________________________ Date ________________

Plural nouns

Bugs, Bushes, and Berries

A singular noun names one person, place, or thing.
A plural noun names more than one.

- Most nouns are made plural by adding s.
- Nouns that end in **s**, **sh**, **ch**, or **x** are made plural by adding **es**.
- Nouns that end in a consonant and **y** are made plural by changing the **y** to an **i** and adding **es**.

Help Ben and Bridget make their way through the maze. Find the singular nouns and change them to plural nouns. Then draw lines to connect those boxes all the way to the balloons. Watch out! The are 12 maze words that are not nouns.

bug bugs	bent	box	bird	baby
bush bushes	berry berries	bell	beautiful	bone
busy	badly	big	because	brush
bench	baboon	body	bike	bear
brain	broken	before	by	baked
bunny	begun	boat	beach	bag
bee	bagel	bus	bold	

Name ______________________ Date ______________

Irregular plural nouns

Strange Plurals!

Most nouns are made plural by adding **s** or **es**.
Quite a few nouns are strange!
Some have special spellings for the plural form.
Example: **person people**
Other nouns have the same singular and plural form.
Example: **fish fish**

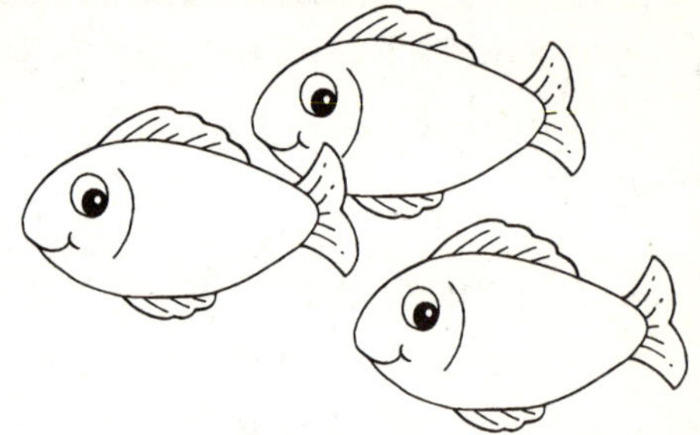

Read the singular noun clues. Write the plural form in the puzzle.
Check the Word Box if you are not sure of your answer.

Across
3. child
5. moose
7. foot
9. goose
11. louse
12. woman

Down
1. mouse
2. man
4. die
6. ox
8. tooth
10. sheep

Word Box

children	feet	lice	mice	oxen	teeth
dice	geese	men	moose	sheep	women

Name ______________________ Date ______________

Pet Day Pandemonium

A noun may show that a person owns or has something. If it is one person, **an apostrophe s ('s)** is added to the end of the name.

Example: **Christopher's cat**

It is pet day in Ms. Zoology's wacky classroom. Fill in possessive nouns for each sentence to complete these tongue twisters. Think of a child's name that begins with the same sound as the animal.

1. Tanya's turtle terrorized ______________ timid tiger.
2. ______________ fast froggy feasted on ______________ fruit flies.
3. ______________ sea lion and ______________ silly seal slowly slid down the slippery slide.
4. ______________ bee buzzed by ______________ baby beagle.
5. ______________ weasel wished it were ______________ wonderful worm.
6. ______________ hamster happily huddled with ______________ harmless hedgehog.
7. ______________ prickly porcupine preferred poking ______________ perfect parakeet.
8. ______________ lizard liked ______________ lovely lobster.

Name ______________________________ Date ______________

Action Words

A verb is a word that names an action. **Glide**, **subtracts**, and **whisper** are verbs.

Read these sentences.
List six different verbs that could fit in each blank.

A. We ________ in our classroom.

1. ______________
2. ______________

3. ______________

4. ______________

5. ______________
6. ______________

B. Never ________ a grizzly bear.

1. ______________
2. ______________
3. ______________
4. ______________
5. ______________
6. ______________

C. Watch out! That dragon wants to

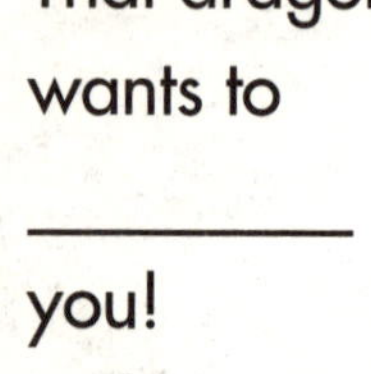

________ you!

1. ______________
2. ______________
3. ______________
4. ______________
5. ______________
6. ______________

D. I like to ________ with my family.

1. ______________

2. ______________
3. ______________

4. ______________
5. ______________

6. ______________

Name ______________________________ Date ________________

Meet Too-Tall Tootsie

Most verbs name actions. The verb *be* is different. It tells about someone or something. **Am**, **is**, and **are** are forms of the verb *be*.

- Use **is** with one person, place, or thing.
- Use **are** with more than one or with the word you.
- Use **am** with the word I.

Write **am**, **is**, or **are** to finish these sentences.

1. My name ______ Too-Tall Tootsie.
2. I _______ 12 feet tall.
3. My hair ______ taller than you _______ !
4. It ______ fun to be tall.
5. I _______ very good at sports.
6. My favorite games _______ volleyball and basketball.
7. Do you know who that ______ on my head?
8. That ______ my twin brother Tiny.
9. We _______ not identical twins!
10. Tiny and I _______ best buddies, however.
11. I _______ friends with most animals.
12. Tiny ______ afraid of birds.
13. They _______ annoying—always trying to use Tiny to build their nests!
14. _______ you afraid of any animals?

Name ______________________ Date ______________

In the Past

Present tense verbs tell about actions happening now.
Past tense verbs tell about actions that happened in the past.
Most verbs are made past tense by adding **ed**.

Add **ed** to make these verbs past tense.

1. help helped
2. play ______
3. rain ______
4. fix ______
5. ask ______
6. visit ______
7. cook ______
8. jump ______

These verbs end in **e**. Just add **d** to make them past tense.

9. change changed
10. rule ______
11. joke ______
12. live ______
13. hike ______
14. dance ______
15. divide ______
16. skate ______

These verbs end in a consonant and **y**.
Change the **y** to **i** and then add **ed** to make them past tense.

17. try tried
18. bully ______
19. spy ______
20. multiply ______
21. study ______
22. marry ______

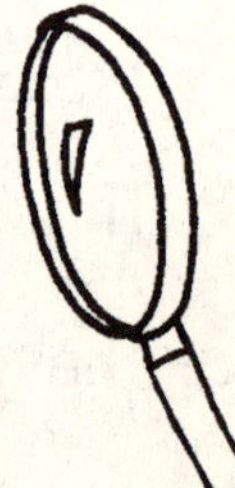

Name ______________________ Date ______________

"Goed" or Went?

Most verbs are made past tense by adding **ed**.
Today I play. Yesterday I played. I have always played.

The verbs in the chart below are tricky. Most change a little, some change a lot. One doesn't change at all! Fill in the missing verbs to see which ones you know.

Present tense (Today I . . .)	**Past tense** (Yesterday I . . .)	**Past tense with a helping verb** (I have/had . . .)
am	was	been
begin		begun
break	broke	
bring		brought
choose	chose	
cut		cut
	drank	drunk
eat		eaten
	flew	flown
give		given
go	went	
know	knew	
run		run
see		seen
think	thought	
take	took	
write		written

Name ______________________ Date ______________

Make a Mini-Book

An adjective is a word that describes a noun.

Read the sample adjectives for each category.
Write several more of your own.
Cut and staple the pages to make a mini-book.
Illustrate a few adjectives in each set on the back of the page before it.
Use the mini-book as a source of interesting words for your own writing.

Name ______________ My Mini-book of **Adjectives**	**Color** 1 turquoise brown colorless silvery
Size, Shape, or Surface 2 enormous triangular shiny	**Number** 3 million three few
Sound, Smell, or Taste 4 thunderous stinky delicious	**Feelings** 5 delighted jealous hopeful proud

Name ______________________________ Date ______________

A Sea, An Ocean

An **article** is a type of adjective.
It signals a noun is coming in a sentence.
The words a, an, and the are articles.

A and **an** describe singular nouns.
A is used if the next word begins with a consonant sound.
An is used if the next word begins with a vowel sound.

Choose the correct article **a** or **an** to use before each ocean animal.

1. a flying fish
2. an angelfish
3. ______ walrus
4. ______ sea lion
5. ______ seal
6. ______ bottle-nosed dolphin
7. ______ Irrawaddy dolphin
8. ______ eagle ray
9. ______ manta ray
10. ______ giant squid
11. ______ octopus
12. ______ beluga whale
13. ______ humpback whale
14. ______ orca
15. ______ crab
16. ______ lobster
17. ______ clam
18. ______ otter
19. ______ sea otter
20. ______ dragonfish
21. ______ electric eel
22. ______ Atlantic cod
23. ______ swordfish
24. ______ icefish
25. ______ tuna
26. ______ seahorse
27. ______ oarfish
28. ______ great white shark

Name ______________________ Date ____________

Comparative and superlative adjectives

Meet the Murrays

Adjectives that compare two people or things often end in **er**.
Adjectives that compare more than two people or things often end in **est**.
I am silly. My sister is sillier than I am. My friend Amy is the silliest person I know.

Read these sentences. Fill in the circle beside the correct missing adjective. Then use the clues to label the five children—Tara, Jason, Zach, Kylie, and Mike.

 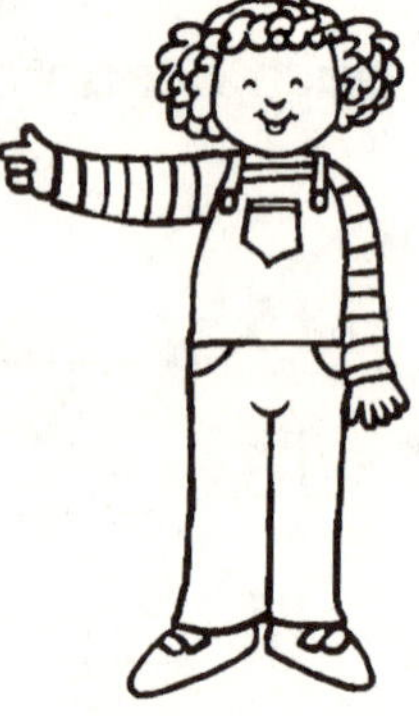   

__________ __________ __________ __________ __________

1. Zach is the _____ one in the family.
   ◯ younger ◯ youngest

2. Kylie is _____ than Jason.
   ◯ younger ◯ youngest

3. Even though Mike is the _____ of all the kids, he is not the tallest.
   ◯ older ◯ oldest

4. Tara is _____ than Mike.
   ◯ tall ◯ taller

5. Tara is usually _____ than Kylie.
   ◯ happier ◯ happiest

6. Zach is a _____ baby.
   ◯ happy ◯ happier

7. Jason is the _____ child of all.
   ◯ happier ◯ happiest

8. Jason is _____.
   ◯ loud ◯ louder

9. Zach is _____ than Jason.
   ◯ louder ◯ loudest

10. Kylie is the _____ kid of all.
   ◯ louder ◯ loudest

Name ______________________ Date ______________

Dress Up Day

A noun names a person, place, or thing.
A pronoun is a word that can take the place of a noun.
I, **you**, **he**, **she**, **it**, **we**, and **they** are pronouns.

Read this story Kathy wrote.
Write the noun each boldfaced pronoun replaces.

1. Kathy and her class
2. ______________
3. ______________
4. ______________
5. ______________
6. ______________
7. ______________
8. ______________
9. ______________
10. ______________

My class has been studying Colonial Life. Today **we** had Dress Up Day. Each student came dressed as a famous colonial person. My teacher, Mr. Wong, even dressed up. **He** was Sam Adams.

I was George Washington. I wore a cape, a white shirt, breeches, and shiny shoes. The best part of my costume was my hat. **It** was a tricorn hat that I got at Colonial Williamsburg last year. My mom helped me fix it. **She** cut two strips of white paper. **We** curled them and taped them inside the hat. **They** looked just like Washington's hair.

We had to tell about the person we were pretending to be. George Washington married Martha Custis when he was 26. **She** was a wealthy widow. Washington did many things in his life. **He** was a surveyor, a farmer, a general, a legislator, and the first President!

Name ______________________________ Date ______________

"You Be the Teacher" Day

The pronouns **you**, **me**, **him**, **her**, **it**, **us**, and **them** can take the place of nouns. They follow action words or words like **to**, **on**, and **with**. Read the story. Write the missing pronouns. Use each word from the box once.

Word Box	me	you	him	her	it	us	them

Today was "You Be the Teacher" Day in our class. Everyone got to teach a lesson. Megan and Carmen went first. They showed ______ how to make toy rockets. We got to launch ________ outside. Most rockets flew about five feet into the air.

Paul went next. He taught us how to say these words in French: Hello, goodbye, thank _______ , and you're welcome. Ms. Gray asked ______ how he learned French. Paul said his grandma is from Haiti and she speaks French.

Soon it was my turn. I taught the class how to draw a shark. I showed them how to make _____ scary-looking. Ms. Gray asked _______ if I could draw any other ocean animals. I told ________ I am learning how to draw whales.

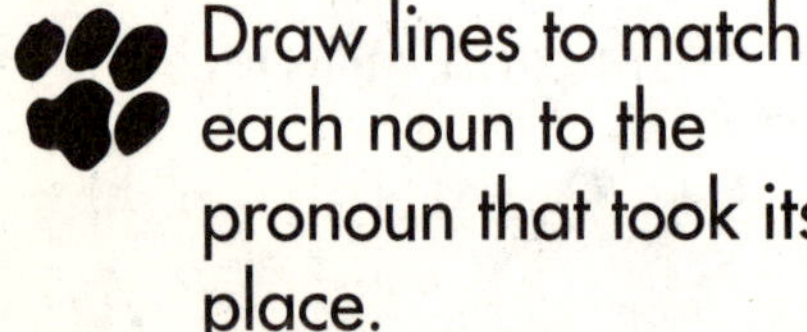

Draw lines to match each noun to the pronoun that took its place.

Nouns	Pronouns
Paul •	• her
Ms. Gray •	• it
the shark •	• them
my classmates and me •	• him
the toy rockets •	• us

Name ______________________________ Date ________________

E-Mail Me!

Read these e-mail messages. Write the missing pronouns.

1. Use **me**, **I**, and **we**.

Dear Casey,

_____ got your e-mail. When does your school year end? ________ get out next week. Write ________ back!

Your cousin,

Jamie

2. Use **you**, **I**, and **it**.

Jamie,

________ am already done with school! ________ ended last Friday. What are ________ doing this summer?

Casey

3. Use **she**, **you**, **I**, **me**, and **it**.

Casey,

Sam and ______ are going to Grandma and Grandpa's house for a week in July. Ask your mom if ________ can come, too. I hope _______ will let you. :) Do you know what :) means? Look at ______ sideways. It's a smiley face. Sam taught ________ that.

Jamie

Name ______________________ Date ______________

Think of the Opposite!

An adverb is a word that describes an action.

Some adverbs tell how. They often end in **ly**.

Andrea **boldly** raised her hand. Bobby juggles **well**.
Andrea **timidly** raised her hand. Bobby juggles **badly**.

 Read each adverb. Write an adverb that means the opposite.

1. quietly ______________
2. sloppily ______________
3. politely ______________
4. carelessly ______________
5. wisely ______________
6. sadly ______________
7. quickly ______________
8. clumsily ______________

Some adverbs tell when an action takes place.

I woke up **early**. I woke up **late**.

 Read each adverb. Write an adverb that means the opposite.

9. always ______________
10. tomorrow ______________
11. soon ______________
12. before ______________
13. rarely ______________

Name ______________________ Date ______________

What's Missing?

A conjunction is a word that connects words, phrases, or sentences. **And**, **or**, **but**, **yet**, and **so** are conjunctions.

Read these sentences. Each one is missing a conjunction—either **and** or **or**. Rewrite the sentence correctly.

1. My friend Laura I are going to the beach.

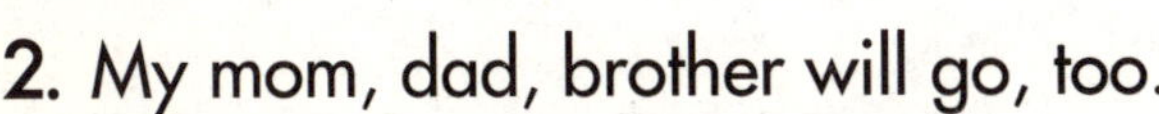

____

2. My mom, dad, brother will go, too.

____

3. We will bring lunch, sunscreen, towels, our bodyboards.

____

____

4. First I want to either swim in the water float on my bodyboard.

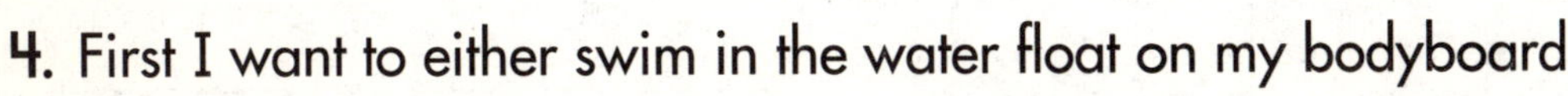

____

____

5. Later, Laura, my brother, I will play in the sand.

____

6. We will build a sandcastle bury each other in the sand.

____

____

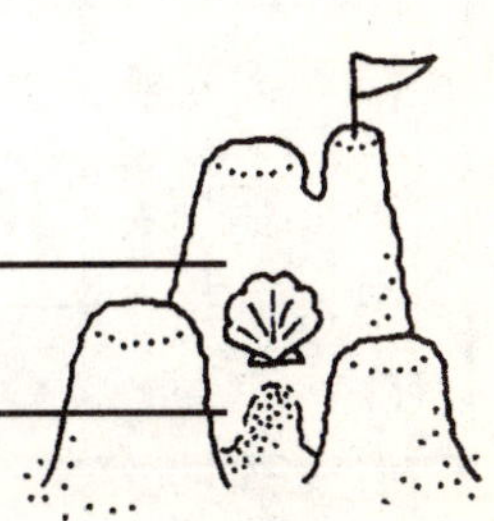

Under, Over, In Front Of . . .

A preposition is a word or set of words that shows the relation between a noun and another word. **In**, **on**, **next to**, **at**, **for**, **with**, and **by** are all prepositions.

Find and circle the 13 prepositions in this puzzle.
All the words go across.
Each would fit in this silly sentence:

I am running _______ a dinosaur!

Write the words on the matching lines next to their row.

i	s	h	o	w	i	t	h	e	s	e
n	o	t	o	w	a	r	d	o	o	r
h	e	l	p	u	b	e	h	i	n	d
p	i	n	s	i	d	e	t	r	e	e
u	s	t	a	r	o	u	n	d	a	y
d	u	n	d	e	r	n	e	a	t	h
m	y	o	v	e	r	t	q	u	a	p
s	h	o	a	w	a	y	f	r	o	m
s	t	e	g	o	b	e	s	i	d	e
b	e	n	e	a	r	y	h	u	g	e
t	y	r	r	a	n	o	n	t	o	y
i	t	t	h	r	o	u	g	h	a	x
m	a	l	o	n	g	s	i	d	e	r

with

_ _ _ _ _ _

_ _ _ _ _ _

_ _ _ _ _ _

_ _ _ _ _ _

_ _ _ _ _ _ _ _ _ _

_ _ _ _

_ _ _ _ _ _ _ _

_ _ _ _ _ _

_ _ _ _

_ _ _ _

_ _ _ _ _ _ _

_ _ _ _ _ _ _ _ _

Name ______________________ Date ______________

Wow! Yikes! Hooray! Oh, No!

An interjection is a word or phrase that shows strong feeling. **Yippee**, **ugh**, **cool**, **gosh**, **good grief**, **aaagh**, **ouch**, and **yowza** are interjections.

Look at these children. Think about their facial expressions and how they might be feeling. Write a caption for each that begins with an interjection.

Whoa! Did you see that?

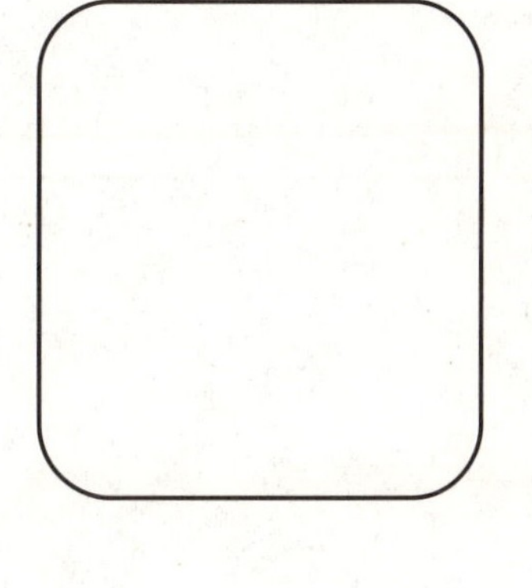

Name ______________________________ Date ______________

Mixed practice

The Parts-of-Speech Patrol

Search through a book you are reading for unusual or appealing nouns, adjectives, verbs, and adverbs. Find 12 words in all and at least two words for each category.

Title ______________________________

Author ______________________________

Nouns (name people, places, or things)

dungeon

traitor

Adjectives (describe nouns)

restless

magnificent

Verbs (action words)

cherished

betray

Adverbs (describe verbs)

proudly

scornfully

Answers

Page 3

Crossed-out nouns:

1. visited
2. happy
3. hunted
4. far
5. cloudy
6. slower
7. tiny
8. carefully
9. drove
10. loud
11. beside
12. spends
13. please
14. healthy
15. clever
16. swims

Page 4

Underlined nouns:

1. school
2. teacher
3. friends
4. person
5. city
6. state
7. dog
8. character
9. author
10. president
11. street
12. month
13. holiday
14. mountain
15. planet

Page 5

Maze plural nouns in order:
bugs, bushes, berries, bells, boxes, birds, babies, bones, brushes, bears, bikes, bodies, baboons, benches, brains, bunnies, bees, bagels, buses, boats, beaches, bags

Page 6

				[1]m				[2]m	
		[3]c	h	i	l	[4]d	r	e	n
				c		i		n	
[5]m	[6]o	o	s	e		c			
	x				[7]f	e	e	[8]t	
[9]g	e	e	[10]s	e				e	
	n		h		[11]l	i	c	e	
			e					t	
[12]w	o	m	e	n				h	
			p						

Page 7

Possessive nouns will vary.

Page 8

Verbs will vary.

Page 9

1. is
2. am
3. is; are
4. is
5. am
6. are
7. is
8. is
9. are
10. are
11. am
12. is
13. are
14. Are

Page 10

1. helped
2. played
3. rained
4. fixed
5. asked
6. visited
7. cooked
8. jumped

---

9. changed
10. ruled
11. joked
12. lived
13. hiked
14. danced
15. divided
16. skated

---

17. tried
18. bullied
19. spied
20. multiplied
21. studied
22. married

Page 11

Present	Past	Past with helping verb
am	**was**	been
begin	**began**	begun
break	broke	**broken**
bring	**brought**	brought
choose	chose	**chosen**
cut	**cut**	cut
drink	drank	drunk
eat	**ate**	eaten
fly	flew	flown
give	**gave**	given
go	went	**gone**
know	knew	**known**
run	**ran**	run
see	**saw**	seen
think	thought	**thought**
take	took	**taken**
write	**wrote**	written

Page 12

Adjectives will vary.

Answers

Page 13

1. a
2. an
3. a
4. a
5. a
6. a
7. an
8. an
9. a
10. a
11. an
12. a
13. a
14. an
15. a
16. a
17. a
18. an
19. a
20. a
21. an
22. an
23. a
24. an
25. a
26. a
27. an
28. a

Page 14

Children in order from left to right:
Kylie, Tara, Zach, Mike, Jason

1. youngest
2. younger
3. oldest
4. taller
5. happier
6. happy
7. happiest
8. loud
9. louder
10. loudest

Page 15

1. Kathy and her class
2. Mr. Wong
3. Kathy
4. Kathy's hat
5. Kathy's mom
6. Kathy and her mom
7. the paper strips
8. Kathy and her class
9. Martha Custis
10. George Washington

Page 16

They showed **us** . . .
We got to launch **them** . . .
Hello, goodbye, thank **you** . . .
Ms. Gray asked **him** . . .
I showed them how to make **it** . . .
Ms. Gray asked **me** . . .
I told **her** . . .

Nouns	Pronouns
Paul •	• her
Ms. Gray •	• it
the shark •	• them
my classmates and me •	• him
the toy rockets •	• us

Page 17

1. **I** got your e-mail. . . **We** get out . . . Write **me** back!
2. **I** am already . . . **It** ended last . . . What are **you** doing . . .
3. Sam and **I** are . . . Ask your mom if **you** can . . . I hope **she** will let you. . . Look at **it** . . . Sam taught **me** that.

Page 18

1. loudly
2. neatly
3. rudely
4. carefully
5. foolishly
6. happily
7. slowly
8. gracefully
9. never
10. yesterday
11. later
12. after
13. frequently

Page 19

1. My friend Laura **and** I are going to the beach.
2. My mom, dad, **and** brother will go, too.
3. We will bring lunch, sunscreen, towels, **and** our bodyboards.
4. First I want to either swim in the water **or** float on my bodyboard.
5. Later, Laura, my brother, **and** I will play in the sand.
6. We will build a sandcastle **or** bury each other in the sand. (Both **and** and **or** are correct.)

Page 20

with
toward
behind
inside
around
underneath
over
away from
beside
near
onto
through
alongside

Page 21

Answers will vary.

Page 22

Answers will vary.